Front page image: courtesy of pixabay.com

"Two roads diverged in a wood, and I —
I took the one less traveled by,
And that has made all the difference."

- The Road Not Taken
by Robert Frost

Ace on the Road?

Vol. 1

A short collection of original poems

by

Bhavin Trivedi

Published 2016

Table of Contents

Rewrite All This

Come on everybody, strap yourselves in.
come on get ready, we're about to begin
to tell the stories and absolve my sin
The road is unknown, I've never been
the destination, it's so hard to pin

I set out only with the books in my head
down a road, that was already well-tread
thinking, that's all I need to get ahead
So easy it was, to spin my own thread
The future's so bright, I'll be well-fed

But to fear, I so desperately clung
like a mother suckling her young
facing fake dangers so far flung
my life in the balance, so faintly hung
and still, i could never find my tongue

Searching life below, searching above
for anything, that could look like love
Despair, disdain, even death were the gov
And benign spirits, couldn't deliver the dove
I'm still out, looking for the meaning of

The one true face, the role that I play
Is it my core, or does it just sway
My heart can be gold, and sometimes just clay
Depends on her, or depends on pay
Need to focus hard, keep my feelings at bay

And as I go on, I would be so remiss
To forget that the future, in motion it is
Feeling a punch, when I wanted a kiss
Always been that way, ever, ever since
Despite yesterday, I can still rewrite all this

199

Ever since I was a young boy,
they were all so nice to me
But really they were out to destroy
any talent that would be

Although I always took it on the chin,
much like a wolverine I was fierce
My secret weapon has always been,
a heart that no one could pierce

Winning and success were elusive,
my achievements were not to be
The cheers and shouts were abusive,
even off-the-field was no remedy

With the help of some who cared,
I was introduced to some teams
But almost none of them dared,
and hastily hollowed out my dreams

With a tiniest glint of hope,
from the down-to-Earth Midwest
Came a lifeline with long rope,
allaying my fears to rest

But after I arrived to this fabled school,
I discovered that the job was not mine
They tried to play me for a fool,
and I was too fragile, so I got in line

False hopes were around the corner lurkin',
it didn't matter the name of the schools
Unfair as it always has been workin',
life still obliged by playground rules.

I was cast out wildly into the real world,
like some smelly rotten piece of ham
My victories were belittled and unfurled,
and no one gave a damn

Everyone was always doubting me,
never was gonna get to The Dance
They were all too blind to see,
just gutless to give me a chance.

Sayin' can't do this, can't do that,
always making some excuses
Treating me like some doormat,
they were just lighting my fuses

One day, destiny put me on the field,
they were given no choice
My take-charge training I did wield,
but still had to wait to rejoice

Eventually I climbed up Everest,
but still I'm not through
I'm going to be the exorcist,
my enemies I will subdue

From the earliest days of dawn,
with all my might, I had declared
That with my brain and brawn,
no one will be spared

People may think that my life,
every step has been a cinch
I may not have known true strife,
but I've fought for every inch

No one figured out about me,
It's not the money, not the game
With all my might, I do decree
You WILL know my name

Get out of Dodge

Out in the cattle country,
amongst the chaff and wheat,
Stood a tiny town
whose rep no one could meet

Guns, games and girls abounded,
Their reputation the world's best,
A sybaritic oasis in the prairie
Vegas of the Old West

After a hard day of riding,
imbibing whiskey to drunken delight,
melt the worries away and
cozy up to the ladies of the night

She looked down from above,
her crystal blue eyes lit up the room,
I threw her a timid smile
And then she lowered the boom

She blew me a precious kiss,
one that I could never expect,
I lost all of my senses
With immediate effect

This way, that way, all the way,
I would succumb to her gladly
I knew too well but didn't care that,
This could only end badly

My palms sweating, my heart pounding,
At the bar, she sidled up to me
Up close, I wanted her so bad,
That my mind began to agree

Considering where I currently was,
I decided to roll the dice
She was just too much to resist,
It was time to start a new vice

I justified my lustful actions
as pursuing a righteous cause
the loving reactions continued,
without any sane pause

In flashes of rapid lightning,
I could no longer control,
My emotional reckoning
worked its weakening toll

Her image could not escape,
my sleeping and awake thought
No matter what my conscience tried,
Like a dead fish i was caught

Her parlor talk and untamed body,
I could not start to dislodge
The only option left to me was,
time to get out of Dodge

Life is not a formula

Narrow and so certain,
I follow the straight line.
While the axioms of life
demonstrate the divine.

The way forward is easy,
everything is set in stone.
Big money, status and love,
will worship my bone.

As I apply the equations,
solving for x, solving for y
There's only one answer
Don't even try to deny

All the rules we must follow,
laid out so long ago.
They're not so arbitrary,
I probably should know.

Through time tested pain,
they've guided me a while.
Serving my highs and lows,
with clarity and guile.

In the realm of reality,
I start to break down.
No more precious proofs,
to solve my feckless frown.

As I sit under this tree,
falling on my head Newton's apple
forces me to reconsider
my thoughts and ideas I grapple

You are not red, and I am not blue

Do you remember a time long ago
when the world was free of worry
As kids we laughed and played
and we were never in a hurry
Nothing was separate or alone
all meals together, even holidays too
Because you are not red,
and I am not blue

While the world evolved so fast,
it didn't change on a dime
But still we truly reel from,
no more 'once upon a time'
It was an illusion anyway,
so the threats can't feel new
Because you are not red,
and I am not blue

Others who arrive to our shores
will act and be different from us
But they don't steal our lives,
it does no good to raise a fuss
Your anger is real, but misguided,
You know that to be true
Because you are not red,
and I am not blue

You may believe you'ro right
to be able to carry your guns
But really all we want is to,
safeguard our daughters and sons
Let's focus on that together,
hand in hand, me and you
Because you are not red,
and I am not blue

The architects of exaggeration
slyly shove their deals of diction
Lulling us further into fear rooms,
located in their fortresses of fiction
Let's not sling the same words
as if we are on cue
Because you are not red,
and I am not blue

We all live under the same roof,
trying to make an honest living
Hatred will get us no where,
we must learn to be forgiving
Life is hard enough,
just trying to get through
Know you are not red,
and I am not blue

Have we fallen to the precipice
of another Civil War
Is it inevitable that
our disgust only asks for more
Our differences are real,
but we should not misconstrue
That you are not red,
and I am not blue

Users

At the first time,
I won her with rhyme,
Words and body, so sublime
I could commit any crime

I wasn't a liar,
and truth led to the mire
my love began to tire
so we couldn't go higher

Never did know,
how to go with the flow
So her animosity did grow
To give me the blow

Finally at last,
she took me to task
for wearing a mask
so i reached for my flask

Pain replaced pleasure
Measure for measure,
With infinite leisure
She depleted my treasure

No hope at all

Some years ago we felt so lucky,
Living in a country so lush and green
Full of wealth and nature so pristine
Prosperity was at beck and call
Never once thought,
No hope at all

The past so bright, led by fat leaders,
But not long ago, the rich men laid it all to waste
They spent the future, with selfish haste
All was forced to fall,
Now there is,
No hope at all

In this vacuum, stepped up some liars
They came from the poor, or maybe the hills
promising freedom, yet making the kills
Yelling their rallying call,
There never will be
No hope at all

Town by town, they burned down the lives
Telling the people, they don't need to learn
Especially the women, who never got their turn
As they ran into the wall
They silently screamed
No hope at all

Body by body, they gathered the flesh
Chopping it up, littering the fields
No force on Earth, to it it yields
Gathering in the hall
As it all diminishes
No hope at all

With no pens, forget about books
They all go to learn, only to endure
In a corrugated box, with only dirt for a floor
The children want only a ball
But there always will be,
No hope at all

As the sun set, crushed everyone's lives
The pain that they all can feel
Hits to the marrow, it's all too real
The night will cast its pall
where the only dream is,
No hope at all

Shallow

I met her so long ago,
in a city that never sleeps.
Money rules over all,
everybody plays for keeps

Smoking on the avenues,
drinking at clubs of jazz.
Late into the night,
hypnotize my body has

Living large on my own terms,
never did I feel this way
So lame, so pathetic,
That's why they call it a cliche

But she cast her spell on me,
she knew what she was doing
I was so powerless
I spent all my money wooing

She wrapped herself on me,
making me feel cool
But then in the end,
She played me for a fool

She whispered sweet nothings,
into my innocent ears.
I mistook them for love
For so many wasted years.

Even though I was strong,
she looked into my eyes
pierced my walls of Troy
Seeding her men of lies

Shameless and shallow,
she lied with infinite glee.
She took all my money,
but I took her dignity.

Cold, lone years have passed,
memories did naturally accrue
Now the story goes that,
she's just someone I knew

If she were the last woman,
on our Earth let's pretend.
And if I was the last man,
the human race would duly end.

Arranged for life

One slow cloudy day in the fall,
I asked them to tell me their story
With a wistful look on their faces,
what they said was devoid of any glory

He had never ever seen her before,
until the morning of their wedding day
When she appeared and showed her face
He realized that he'd rather be on his way

A desperate thought with a sunken heart,
but he felt he could never flee
No matter how hard he could try
Because he knew, she was his destiny

But the deal was even worse for her,
she had no choice in any shape or form
All she thought she could safely do,
was pray each day to weather the storm

When the fateful day finally arrived
the families and townsfolk were so thrilled
Excitement for everyone else but them,
But they tried so hard to not feel so killed

Paraded like a colorful porcelain statue
She was forced to remain demure,
Shutting down all her senses so that,
The ceremony passed by like one big blur

As if standing at the edge of a cliff,
the thought of forever caused him to rankle
Perhaps she sensed the unease in him,
So she showed him some flashes of ankle

Only to the most arrogant of minds,
would this have been a curse.
With careful thought and deliberate action,
into their lives *together,* did they immerse

As the decades trudged on and life happened,
who knows of interventions from above
But one thing became clear between them,
they did grow one kind of true love

Never can go home again

Ever since he was a young boy so poor
He couldn't wait to leave his parents' door
Working well into the dark night with his pen,
he never dreamed to go home again

The elder ones had fab stories they told,
of a distant land that was paved with gold
so got busy trying to prove that he was men,
he didn't know, that one never can go home again

He landed in the city, ambled around like a fool,
what he needed to learn, could not be done in school
Discovered the world of booze and babes, oh amen!
There's no way that he'd ever go home again

One day, she danced her way into life
wishing this innocent would make her his wife
to his virgin eyes she was a model ten
he felt ready, never wanted to go home again

But then he realized that he was still a Brahmin
Dictating that they had, nothing left in common
How would he one day explain back home to Jen
He was terrified to face up and go home again

With swigs of spirits and fancy clothes worn,
he realized that this new life was lonely and forlorn
walking around like a cub far from its den
he was lost, as one never can go home again

He couldn't relate to anyone or get the gist
like the digit fingers, separated from the fist
never did he care to learn, who knows when
that one never can go home again

Beaten down, as the stranger in a strange land
feeling defeated, like Custer at his Last Stand
In a flash, ready to give it all up right there and then,
He knew too well, that he never can go home again

A Walk in the Shire

I followed you to this ancient place
so full of future, yet stuck in the past
There is so much potential here
but the people go nowhere fast
You could fight them today, everyday
But instead of wallowing in the mire,
let's forget our troubles for the day,
and take a walk in the shire

Having stood for so many centuries,
a land full of cathedrals and castles
Testament to an eternal truth that everyone,
is merely a group of enchained vassals
People should never be any possession,
I never want you to say to me, *yes sire*
As equals of mind and heart, just hold my hand,
and take a walk in the shire

One day the sun was shining so brightly,
illuminating the verdant valleys of wonder
But on the horizon appeared ominous clouds,
we shuddered at the delicate sound of thunder
Oh how and why did we come here
Can we withstand the storms so dire
Maybe if we can see beyond our own self,
and take a walk in the shire

In the daily drivel, it's so easy to forget,
What we have can be a perfect ten,
Working hard we need to know deep down,
that we won't get fooled again
But instead we have allowed ourselves,
to go down to the wire
We have ruefully forgotten how to talk,
and take a walk in the shire

After a progression of long lonely days,
and not always seeing eye to eye
It was time to start asking the hard questions
as we strolled along the River Wye
And as for me, you should already know,
never a special request will you require
Just warmly take my hand always,
and take a walk in the shire

While you may not always get what you want,
consider all the hurdles you have overcome
But with the wits fueled by the fire in your heart,
to the dangers you will not succumb
Of all that you have accomplished,
all that you have won, I will never tire
I invite you to celebrate all the triumphs,
and take a walk in the shire

The lush green rolling hills abounded,
inspired Tolkien to be ever so clever
sprinkled as far as the eye could see,
were succulent strawberry fields forever
Any way we would turn to look afar,
Views in all directions that never tire,
Inclined us to ease our cold conscience,
and take a walk in the shire

We must be weary after so many years,
before time marches too far as we get old
We can't afford to waste another day more,
let us glide together across these fields of gold
But I ignore the everlasting beauty around,
As there is so much of you to admire
I would be honoured if you go willingly with me,
and take a walk in the shire

Ace on the Road?

Early in the morning
before I could even think,
I struggled to open my eyes
so I decided to pour my drink
Very much dearly so
like a river it flowed,
needed to find
the ace on the road

All the things and people
that I once knew,
I shuddered to realize
were no longer so true
The schemers and liars
use their expertise to goad,
making me feel like I'm
the ace on the road

With temptation tapping at every door,
the way forward is never a straight line,
clouded by pleasure, i mistook it as
a search for the divine
Like a crumbling house of cards
I watched my conscience erode,
I sure could use
an ace on the road

I just kept going on and on
like a rolling ramble,
Learning that each step of life
is really just a gamble
But as the hopes and dreams
began to implode,
while desperately seeking
an ace on the road

Everything was getting lost
with all that I did so hard to try,
There was no way out,
even money couldn't buy
It was easier to flush it
down the commode,
there was no hope
of any ace on the road

As each day lingered on
I could no longer afford,
It was definitely time
to cut the umbilical cord
No more messin' around
time to change the mode,
I have to get the control
as ace on the road

After hitting rock bottom
and learning that life ain't fair,
I started to realize that
the answers might be out there
As I go on, one place to the next
the problems begin to unload,
but hardly I am
that ace on the road

As the sun reaches high noon
I was getting some traction,
With revolution of thought
and evolution of action
Maybe I shouldn't fear
all that much i had sowed,
bears fruit one day soon
as ace on the road …

About the Writer

Bhavin Trivedi has dabbled in many different jobs over the years including nearly half a decade as a stay-at-home dad. Even though he has been on-call 24/7/365 for that time, he swears that it is the best job anyone could have.

He was born in India, grew up in New Jersey, has lived in New York City, Ann Arbor, Chicago, Oklahoma City, Costa Rica, Nicaragua and England, but now resides in Minnesota with his wife and two children.